The Lost Hawks Cap

By Eliza Webb

Mum, Aubry and Paul walked from school to the park.

Paul seemed sad and withdrawn.

"What's the cause of your frown, Paul?" said Aubry.

Paul started to bawl!

"I lost my Hawks cap!" he said.
"Grandad bought it for me.
I should not have brought it
to school.
It's my fault!"

At the park, Aubry saw Fawn from school.

Fawn was playing on the seesaw. And she had a Hawks cap!

“Fawn has Paul’s Hawks cap!” Aubry thought.

Aubry thought about what to do.

Just then, Aubry saw Mr Moody
run to the park.

He had a Hawks cap
in his hand!

"Paul!" said Mr Moody.
"I saw your cap on the lawn at school!"

Mr Moody launched the cap up high.
Paul caught it.

Then something dawned on Aubry.

“Paul has a Hawks cap, and Fawn does, too!” she said.

"Mum, I thought Fawn was naughty and took Paul's cap," said Aubry.
"This has taught me to think the best of people."

CHECKING FOR MEANING

1. Why did Paul start to bawl? *(Literal)*
2. Who found Paul's cap? *(Literal)*
3. How did Paul feel about losing his Hawks cap? *(Inferential)*

EXTENDING VOCABULARY

withdrawn	Using clues from the story, explain the meaning of the word *withdrawn*. What other words could the author have used?
bought/ brought	What is the difference between the words *bought* and *brought*?
dawned	Think about what happens to the sun at dawn. Now talk about what happened when *something dawned on Aubry*.

MOVING BEYOND THE TEXT

1. What things are precious to you? How do you keep them safe?

2. Aubry thought that Fawn had taken Paul's cap, but then she realised she had made a mistake when she saw that there were two caps. Have you ever jumped to the wrong conclusion about something? What happened?

3. Why is it a good idea to generally think the best of people and not assume they have done something wrong?

4. What do you think would have happened if Aubry had accused Fawn of taking Paul's cap? How would it have affected their friendship?

TIME TO WRITE

Write about your favourite possession and where it came from. Did someone give it to you? Did you buy it with your own money?

PRACTICE WORDS

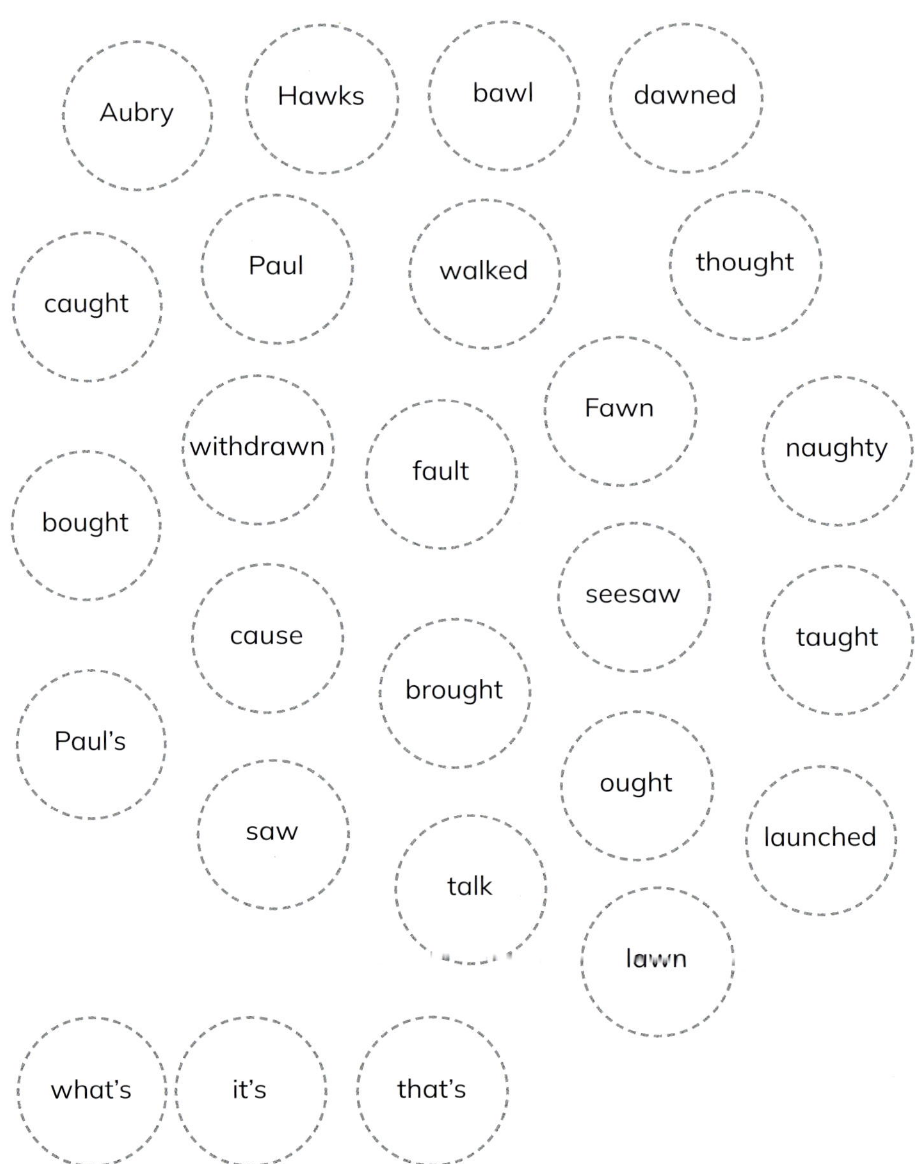